John Francis Davis

Vizier Ali Khan

Or the Massacre of Benares, a Chapter in British Indian History

John Francis Davis

Vizier Ali Khan

Or the Massacre of Benares, a Chapter in British Indian History

ISBN/EAN: 9783743411371

Manufactured in Europe, USA, Canada, Australia, Japa

Cover: Foto ©ninafisch / pixelio.de

Manufactured and distributed by brebook publishing software (www.brebook.com)

John Francis Davis

Vizier Ali Khan

VIZIER ALI KHAN

OR

THE MASSACRE OF BENARES:

A CHAPTER IN

BRITISH INDIAN HISTORY.

'I talk not of mercy, I talk not of fear;
He neither must know who would serve the VIZIER.'
                                                    Byron.

Printed by
SPOTTISWOODE & CO., NEW-STREET SQUARE, LONDON
1871.

PREFACE
TO
THE SECOND EDITION.

THE first appearance of this short History was in 1844, and the whole impression having been long since exhausted, the present renewal, with some additions, in a limited number of copies, is chiefly for the supply of private friends and relatives. The principal details were obtained by me from the late Hon. Mountstuart Elphinstone, appointed on his first arrival in India as assistant to my father the judge and magistrate of Benares, and present at the time of the revolt.

There were episodes in the late Indian Mutiny not unlike the events here recorded. Had the first outbreak at Meerut, in 1857, been as speedily quenched, and the mutinous regiments prevented from marching to Delhi, the perils of that crisis might have been greatly diminished.

Vizier Ali was probably encouraged in his attempt at Benares by the aspect of affairs on the side of Mysore, where Lord Wellesley had been summoned from Calcutta by the war with Tippoo Sultaun, terminated only by the defeat and death of that Prince at Seringapatam in the following May, about four months after the failure of Vizier Ali. Had the latter not been so speedily put down, the spread of revolt at such a period might have taxed the resources of the Indian Government. Lord Wellesley's appreciation of the service rendered at Benares is recorded at page 75, in testimonials from himself.

J. F. D.

VIZIER ALI KHAN

OR

THE MASSACRE OF BENARES.

───◆───

THE kingdom of Oude is the only portion of the great plain of the Ganges that is not immediately subject to the government of British India; extending from the banks of that great river to the foot of the lower range of Himalaya, and surrounded on three of its sides by the dominions of the Company. Lucnow, the capital, though a large and populous place in early times, became the residence of the court as late as 1775, but soon grew to be one of the wealthiest cities in Hindoostan; rivalling those more ancient seats,

> Where the gorgeous East, with richest hand,
> Shower'd on her kings barbaric pearls and gold.

On the decease of the reigning sovereign,

Asoph ul Dowlah, in 1797, the rulers of British India 'were compelled,' said Lord Teignmouth, ' by an extraordinary concurrence of circumstances, to become the arbiters of the disposal of a kingdom.' The claim to succession lay between Vizier Ali, the reputed son of the deceased nawaub, and the lineal descendant of his father Sujah ul Dowlah, by name Saadut Ali. After some deliberation on the respective rights of these two claimants, the decision was made in favour of Vizier Ali, the presumptive eldest son and heir-apparent to the deceased sovereign of Oude. The ground of this decision was his acknowledgment of that youth, now seventeen years of age, as his own son, corroborated by a series of corresponding acts and declarations, and by the sentence of the Mahomedan law, which supported the validity of such a claim.

The reign of the young nawaub was, however, destined to be short. Reports and suspicions, at first so faint that they did not prevent his succession, though they had embarrassed the counsels which confirmed it, gained strength as to the spuriousness of his origin. It was ascertained at length, on indubitable evidence, that Asoph ul Dowlah, who had no sons of his own, had purchased his mother, the wife of a Fraush or menial person, a short time previous to the birth of Vizier Ali, and adopted the child as his own. The abandoned conduct of the youth after his undeserved elevation seemed to argue a spurious and ignoble nature; but he was not long able to abuse the station to which he was so little entitled.

The consciousness of his insecure position probably led to his entertaining those hostile and treacherous designs towards the English which tended only to hasten his downfall. By nature he was fearless, sanguinary, and uncontrollable; in conduct debauched, and unbounded in profusion. His proceedings soon showed that he was determined to maintain his position at all risks—'*et quærere conscius arma.*' Immediately after Vizier Ali's succession to the musnud of Oude, and before any question arose as to his right, the Governor-General of India had planned a visit to Lucnow. Before his arrival, the letters from the British resident at that court stated, what was afterwards proved, the early determination.

of the young nawaub to establish his own power, if possible, by the subversion of the influence of the Company.

On the morning when the intended visit had been intimated through the resident, the state of affairs at Lucnow wore a most alarming appearance. Ten or twelve battalions of troops were called in, the artillery was served with ammunition, and a confederacy formed with hostile designs. The result of his deliberations with his adherents was a letter, described by the resident as requiring for answer either the most implicit acquiescence or the *ultima ratio* of the sword. Shief Ali, the father-in-law of the nawaub, was with difficulty induced to prevail on him to substitute one rather more temperate, and which the governor-general received on his approach from Calcutta.

The particulars communicated by the minister, Zehseen Ali Khan, the secret adherent of the rightful claims of Saadut Ali, were very unfavourable. He stated that the conduct of Vizier Ali since his accession had exhibited a course of meanness, profligacy, and vice. He had avowed to the minister, who urged the obligations of his predecessor to the Company, that he would submit to no dependency. His own expressions, in the letter received from him, sufficiently confirmed this. 'I am confident,' said he, 'that no one will dare to annihilate my authority and dignity.' The minister added, as his own opinion, that if Vizier Ali's power were at all equal to resistance, he would oppose any interference on the part of the British by force; and that he meditated such a course might be inferred from the fact of his exacting oaths from his commanders to be faithful to him.

The measures of Vizier Ali, soon after his accession, had been directed to the degradation of the minister, who was generally considered as favourable to the brother of the late nawaub, and a friend of the English. He repeatedly interdicted, under threats of severe punishment, all persons from attending the disgraced functionary. The official duties of the minister were, by order, absolutely suspended, while Vizier Ali assumed the entire authority over the military, whom he conciliated with the most unbounded profusion. The advice and remonstrance of the British resident were repeated without effect; and the governor-general was subsequently convinced, that nothing but his determination to proceed to Lucnow with a respectable force would have prevented the subversion of the English influence in Oude, or the alternative of hostilities to preserve it.

The approach of Vizier Ali and the governor-general, from Lucnow and Juanpore respectively, bore all the aspect of doubtful friendship. The nawaub had at one time determined to advance with a large force and a numerous train of artillery; but this measure was relinquished at the advice of the mother of the late sovereign, the Begum, or queen-dowager, and he in consequence announced that he should be accompanied by a very small escort. The language of his letters to Sir John Shore was civil and submissive, and such it had been to the resident, at the same time that he was secretly undermining his position. Many respectable persons were deterred from waiting on the governor-general by the fear of offending the nawaub.

Some days after his arrival at Lucnow, Sir John Shore was cautioned, through various channels, not to put his person in the power of Vizier Ali, under the impression that assassination was intended. Information was subsequently communicated that troops to a large amount had been secretly introduced into the town, and that orders had been sent to different battalions to march in. Two actually approached from the neighbourhood; the nawaub admitted the fact, but denied that they came by his orders, and remanded one of them. These circumstances determined the governor-general to quit his residence in the city of Lucnow, and to occupy a garden-house of the nawaub at the distance of about five miles from his residence.

This removal had the apparent effect of alarming the nawaub, who on the following day quitted Lucnow, and encamped at a small distance from the place occupied by the governor-general. He was here attacked by a disorder which prevented his meeting Sir John Shore for a considerable interval, during which the latter had an opportunity of prosecuting inquiries, the result of which led him to say 'that he had never been involved in a scene of greater perplexity and profligacy.'

Almas Ali Khan was a renter of Oude—that is, farmer of the revenue of a large portion of the nawaub's country He was one of that class of persons common in oriental seraglios, and had formerly been attached to Soojah ul Dowlah's zenanah. Hitherto the great friend and supporter of Vizier Ali, and second only to himself in the kingdom of Oude, he had been sedulously watching the progress of things, and, when the house showed symptoms of falling, he prepared to quit it, with the sagacity of that small but astute animal which has given a name to this species of desertion. He called upon the minister, and surprised him with strong complaints of the conduct of the nawaub, whom he loaded with opprobrious invectives. He spoke of him as being at once spurious and profligate, and as calculated to ruin the country by his vices and profusion. He expressed his alarm lest a knowledge of his conduct should reach the governor-general and force him into violent measures. He mentioned the entire approbation of the Begum as to his conduct, and her earnest wish, as well as his own, that Vizier Ali should be deposed, and some one of the sons of Soojah ul Dowlah placed on the musnud. The same was successively repeated by Almas to the governor-general, both alone and in company with the commander-in-chief. He declared that the power of the Begum would be sufficient, in the presence of the English troops, to depose Vizier Ali, and promised a considerable sum in compensation of the acquiescence and aid of the British authorities.

The opinion of Almas as to the defective title of Vizier Ali was consistent with his declarations immediately subsequent to his elevation; and the joint admission of both himself and the Begum, as to his spurious origin, left them without the shadow of a pretext for objecting to the claim of Saadut Ali on the ground of right.

It was at this period that the governor-general deemed it necessary to prepare for the accomplishment of the event, by writing to the resident at Benares, Mr. Cherry, who, as chief judge of the Court of Appeal, was the channel of communication with the foreigners of rank at that city. As Benares was destined to be the scene of the final catastrophe, it becomes necessary to give some account of that ancient Hindoo city.

The district in which it is situated was ceded by the subsidiary treaty of 1775 to the British power by the Nawaub of Oude, Asoph ul Dowlah, in compensation (as was alleged at the time) of the aid which he had received in reducing to subjection one of his tributary chiefs.* The city is built on the north or left bank of the Ganges, as that great river flows eastward, and presents a fine appearance when viewed from the water. The eye rests on a variety of noble buildings, some of them highly ornamented, and with terraces on their summits; while the view is improved by the numerous flights of stone steps which lead from the banks of the river to Hindoo temples, or serve the crowds of devotees in the performance of their frequent ablutions.

Mr. Macaulay has given the following graphic description of 'Benares, a city which in wealth, population, dignity, and sanctity, was among the foremost of Asia. It was commonly believed that half a million of human beings

* The compact in question was in reality a general treaty for furnishing a force to protect him against *all* enemies.

was crowded into that labyrinth of lofty alleys, rich with shrines, and minarets, and balconies, and carved oriels, to which the sacred apes clung by hundreds. The traveller could scarcely make his way through the press of holy mendicants, and not less holy bulls. The broad and stately flights of steps, which descended from these swarming haunts to the bathing-places along the Ganges, were worn every day by the footsteps of an innumerable multitude of worshippers.* The schools and temples drew crowds of pious Hindoos from every province where the Brahminical faith was known. Hundreds of devotees came thither every month to die; for it was believed that a peculiarly happy fate awaited the man who should pass from the sacred city into the sacred river. Nor was superstition the only motive which allured strangers to that great metropolis. Commerce had as many pilgrims as religion. All along the shores of the venerable stream lay great fleets of vessels laden with rich merchandise. From the looms of Benares went forth the most delicate silks that adorned the balls of St. James's and of the

* Appendix A.

Petit Trianon; and in the bazaars, the muslins of Bengal and the sabres of Oude were mingled with the jewels of Golconda and the shawls of Cashmere. This rich capital, and the surrounding tract, had long been under the immediate rule of a Hindoo prince (the Rajah of Benares) who rendered homage to the Mogul emperors. During the great anarchy of India, the lords of Benares became independent of the court of Delhi, but were compelled to submit to the authority of the Nabob of Oude. Oppressed by this formidable neighbour, they invoked the protection of the English. The English protection was given; and at length the Nabob Vizier, by a solemn treaty, ceded all his rights over Benares to the Company. From that time the rajah was the vassal of the government of Bengal, acknowledged its supremacy, and engaged to send an annual tribute to Fort William.'

Benares was of old renowned as the principal seat of Brahminical learning. Robertson, in his History of India, speaks of it as the Athens of the East, the residence of the most learned Brahmins, and the centre of their science and literature; and Sir Robert Barker, an early visitor, has described an observatory there, said to have been erected by the Emperor Akhbar,* in which were astronomical instruments of large dimensions, constructed with great skill and ingenuity. Mr. Davis, who was judge and magistrate of the district about the period of this narrative, and who will be found to perform a conspicuous part towards the conclusion of it, profited by his residence there to investigate the astronomical science of the Brahmins. He was the first Englishman who applied a knowledge of their sacred language to an examination of their books. The results of his researches were discussed by Mr. Cavendish, in the Philosophical Transactions, and are known to all who feel interested in the early history of the science to which they relate.† A Hindoo Sanscrit College, established in the year 1791, and supported by the British government, has continued to prosper to the present day.

* The observatory was really built by Jysingh, Rajah of Jypore, about the year 1700. See Asiatic Researches, vol. v. p. 177.
† Cited by Robertson in his History of India, Note LXVIII.

As the crowded streets of an Asiatic town possess few attractions for Europeans, the residences of the English at Benares are chiefly erected at Secrole, a short distance from the city. In style they somewhat resemble the villas and country seats of our English gentry, with such modifications as may be demanded by the climate. Insulated within their own grounds, the four sides are open to the winds, while a plentiful supply of Venetian blinds serves to exclude the excess of the sun's rays. The height does not generally exceed one story above the ground floor; but the flat roofs afford space for extensive terraces with parapets, which in some cases are approached by narrow winding stairs, surmounted by a trap-door. This mode of construction is particularised here, because it will be found to exercise a considerable influence on succeeding events.

Benares was the scene of one of the most remarkable adventures of Warren Hastings—one in which he rashly exposed himself to great personal peril, but extricated himself with equal resolution and skill. The transaction, which, from its dubious character, formed one of the principal charges against the British proconsul on his return home, was briefly this.

The governor-general had instituted a claim against the Rajah Cheyte Singh of some hundred thousands of pounds sterling, and he followed up the excuses or evasions of the rajah by force. He visited Benares, and there, notwithstanding the personal submissions and protestations of the unfortunate Cheyte Singh, had him arrested by two companies of troops in his own capital. This extreme measure, accompanied as Hastings was by a mere handful of troops, soon led to an insurrection among the subjects of the outraged prince. 'The building,' relates Mr. Macaulay, 'in which he had taken up his residence was on every side blockaded by the insurgents. But his fortitude remained unshaken. The rajah from the other side of the river sent apologies and liberal offers. They were not even answered. Some subtle and enterprising men were found, who undertook to pass through the throng of enemies, and to communicate the intelligence of the late events to the English cantonments. It is the fashion of the natives of India to wear large ear-rings of gold. When they travel, the rings are laid aside, lest the precious metal should tempt some gang of robbers; and, in place of the ring, a quill or a roll of paper is inserted in the orifice to prevent it from closing. Hastings placed in the ears of his messenger letters rolled up in the smallest compass.

'Things, however, were not yet at the worst. An English officer of more spirit than judgment, eager to distinguish himself, made a premature attack on the insurgents beyond the river. His troops were entangled in narrow streets, and assailed by a furious population. He fell, with many of his men, and the survivors were forced to retire. The hopes of Cheyte Singh began to rise. Instead of imploring mercy in the humble style of a vassal, he began to talk the language of a conqueror, and threatened, it was said, to sweep the white usurpers out of the land. But the English troops were now assembling fast. The officers and even the private men regarded the governor-general with enthusiastic attachment, and flew to his aid with an alacrity which, as he boasted, had never been shown on any other occasion. Major Popham, a brave and skilful soldier, who had highly distinguished himself in the Mahratta war, and in whom the governor-general reposed the greatest confidence, took the command. The tumultuary army of the rajah was put to rout. His fortresses were stormed. In a few hours about thirty thousand men left his standard and returned to their ordinary avocations. The unhappy prince fled from his country for ever. His fair domain was added to the British dominions. One of his relatives indeed was appointed rajah; but the Rajah of Benares was henceforth to be, like the Nabob of Bengal, a mere pensioner.'

Such was his condition at the period of this narrative, to which we return. The decision, as to deposing Vizier Ali, being once made, there was no difficulty in fixing on the rightful successor. Saadut Ali, as before stated, was the eldest surviving son of Soojah ul Dowlah, the late nawaub's father. When the treaty proposed by the governor-general was communicated to that prince, 'it was not the time,' as Mill observes, 'to dispute about terms.' His consent being obtained, he was conveyed secretly to Cawnpore,* and once safely arrived

* There was something interesting in the mode of Saadut Ali's journey to Cawnpore. Mr. Cherry ordered relays to be

there, was openly escorted by a large body of European troops from Cawnpore to Lucnow. 'The governor-general committed the peace of the city to the charge of the elder Begum (the late nawaub's mother), whose influence over the turbulent elements of discord now collected within its walls he knew to be paramount; and he moreover enjoined her to be in readiness on the following morning to bestow the *khelaut* of investiture on the rightful heir to the throne; overcoming her reluctance to accept the twofold duty by threatening, in the event of her refusal, to entrust it to other hands. Saadut Ali, as he entered the city at the appointed time, manifested considerable alarm; and, to quiet his fears, Sir John Shore placed him on his own elephant. As they advanced through the streets to the palace, the governor-general amused the immense multitude, assembled to

prepared as for himself, and had his clothes packed in the baskets which accompany a traveller on such occasions. For these baskets, others belonging to Saadut Ali were afterwards privately substituted; he put on a travelling dress, and let it be supposed, when he retired for the night, that he had set off on his journey. Meanwhile Saadut Ali was introduced into his palankeen, and in this he travelled night and day through the territory of his rival as far as Cawnpore, without guard or protection of any kind but his pistols.

witness the inaugural procession, by showering rupees among them, while he did not neglect the opportunity of inculcating on the nabob advice respecting his future conduct.'* As both the disposition of the natives and the power of the British rendered resistance hopeless on the part of Vizier Ali, the rightful nawaub was proclaimed without opposition on the 21st January, 1798.†

In his treaty with the governor-general, he agreed to allow an annual pension of a lac and a half of rupees (£15,000) to the deposed Vizier Ali, whose future residence was to be at Benares. It might perhaps even then, and without any reference to succeeding events, have been questioned how far the measure was prudent of allowing the deposed sovereign to fix his abode just on the frontier of his late domain, and, as it were, 'within hail' of it. The shadow of power which he was allowed to retain, in a most numerous retinue, and certain personal distinctions, was by no means calculated to diminish the risks of future trouble, arising from those natural hankerings which

* Life of Lord Teignmouth, by his son.
† Appendix B.

beset deposed sovereigns, and which (if we may compare together things of very unequal magnitude) so soon brought Napoleon back from Elba.

India, besides, was at this time in a far from settled or comfortable state. Zemaun Shah, the king of the Afghans, and the remaining head of the Mahomedan power in the East, was with a powerful army at Lahore, hanging over our frontier; there were large bodies of French troops with Scindia and the Nizam; and the war with Tippoo Sultaun, which ended in the destruction of the kingdom of Mysore, was on the eve of breaking out; while, in addition to these salient points, there was a general ferment in the minds of the Mussulman princes and nobles, many of whom had but very recently been deprived of power. 'When one looks back,' says a very distinguished Indian governor, in a letter now lying before the writer of this narrative, ' when one looks back on those times, one can hardly believe in the panic (Afghanistan) lately felt in India, which led to so many real dangers and evils.' Sir John Shore, soon after created Lord Teignmouth, had no sooner returned to Calcutta from Lucnow than he embarked to re-

turn home, where his measures regarding Vizier
Ali met with the entire approval of the British
Government and the Court of Directors. The
Marquis Wellesley (then Lord Mornington) arrived in India in May, 1798, and his attention
was immediately occupied by the threatening
aspect of affairs on the side of Mysore. Three
weeks after reaching Calcutta, he received the
intelligence that Tippoo had solicited the aid of
the French in a contemplated scheme to overthrow the British power in the East.

It was in such times that Vizier Ali, who,
during his short reign as sovereign of Oude,
had betrayed a disposition sufficiently restless,
found himself reduced to a comparatively private condition at Benares, and under the surveillance, if not the coercion, of the British
authorities. The house or palace allotted for
his residence was situated in an extensive inclosure, which went by the name of Mahdoo
Doss's Garden, on the outskirts of the city of
Benares. He never issued out thence without
being attended by a numerous armed train of
adherents from Lucnow, and entertained as
many more on the footing of guards as he
thought proper. In addition to this, the ket-

tle-drum or nackára, a mark of high rank, was always carried before him when he went from home.

The two chief civil authorities at Benares were Mr. Cherry, the political agent of the governor-general, and Mr. Davis, judge and magistrate of the district and city court. The natural disposition of Vizier Ali, joined to his peculiar position, rendered him little inclined to cultivate an acquaintance with the British inhabitants of Benares; but the peculiar functions of Mr. Cherry, as the agent of the supreme government in relation to that individual, rendered some personal intercourse and an interchange of visits indispensable. With this exception, the deposed nawaub held no communication with a single European.

Unhappily for Mr. Cherry, he was little disposed to entertain any suspicions of sinister designs on the part of his charge, or to apprehend that Vizier Ali was at all likely to abuse that indulgence which permitted him to be surrounded with the retinue and the forms of an independent prince. Recent disasters in the East (since so well retrieved by the disciplined valour of our troops) have exemplified the fatal results of a similar confidence on the part of a great public functionary, who unhappily paid but too dearly for miscalculating the depths of Asiatic treachery.

Opportunities had occurred to Mr. Davis, as head of the civil government of Benares, to become cognizant of the suspicious conduct and disposition of Vizier Ali. He had warned Mr. Cherry, as well as the supreme government at Calcutta, of the consequences that might be anticipated. 'One measure of precaution,' he observed, 'might be to remove from the city and district all the Mahomedans whose high rank and ample incomes may be supposed to inspire them with ambitious views, and who might possibly be induced to throw their weight into the scale of insurrection.' It was hardly necessary (he added) to observe that he alluded in particular to Mahomedan pensioners, for whom the city of Benares, situated on the frontier, and dedicated to Hindoo religion, seemed, of all places in the Company's provinces, the least fitted as a residence.

In fact, should a struggle with the government take place, there were many persons in different parts of the district whose attachment to the British interests was not such as would prevent their joining the side that possessed any chance of being successful, especially were money to be readily distributed. 'I should be sorry,' observed the judge of Benares, in his letters to Calcutta, 'to find that any observations of mine had tended to lessen the accommodations and indulgences afforded by government to the parties in question; though, at the same time, I cannot refrain from avowing my hearty wish that those accommodations and indulgences were afforded to them in some other place than Benares; or at least that their armed followers were reduced, and their cannon and other warlike implements deposited among the military apparatus of government.'

It could never have appeared to the native inhabitants that Vizier Ali resided at Benares in a private capacity. The external marks of high rank which he always exhibited, the maintenance of guards, horse and foot, in his own pay, without control or limitation, joined to the demeanour of defiance displayed by himself and attendants to the civil power on every possible occasion, were circumstances which served not only to cherish views of independence in himself, but to impress others with the probability of his acquiring it. They were, moreover, calculated to induce certain persons of rank residing within the British provinces, but disaffected to the government, more readily to enter into his views of re-establishment in the dominion of Oude; an object which subsequent occurrences proved he never had relinquished. He had sent a vackeel (or envoy) to Zemaun Shah, he possessed an active agent at Calcutta, and was, besides, in correspondence with persons devoted to his interest in different parts of Bengal.

It also appeared that he had looked forward to the much talked of invasion of India by the Afghans, under Zemaun Shah, as a favourable opportunity for manifesting his designs, and had engaged some of the principal people of Benares to afford him assistance whenever he should attempt open insurrection. Though these intrigues were carried on with considerable diligence and success by Vizier Ali and the two companions of his youthful follies and vices, by name Izzut Ali and Waris Ali, there can be no doubt that the ultimate execution of their project was to depend on the expected operations of Zemaun Shah, and the employment which the British forces were likely to find on the western frontiers of Oude in the expected invasion.

The main army to the westward was under the command of General Sir James Craig, while, unfortunately for Vizier Ali and his ambitious projects, there was a reserve, under Major-General Erskine, encamped within a short march of the city of Benares. It would be manifestly ill-timed in him to declare himself as long as such a state of things existed; but a crisis in his affairs arose, which hardly left him the choice of deliberation.

The original error of placing the deposed nawaub at Benares being repeatedly brought to the notice of government, began, towards the conclusion of the first year of his residence there, to excite its serious attention; and Mr. Cherry was at length instructed to convey to Vizier Ali the resolution of the governor-general, Lord Mornington, to remove him to Calcutta. This announcement, as might be expected, fell like a thunder-stroke on one who was engaged in organising schemes which, if successful, would soon render him independent, if not again a sovereign. To be compelled to reside in the immediate vicinity, and under the supervision of the supreme government, was a death-blow to all chances of success from insurrectionary projects. His remonstrances were loud and urgent, but they proved vain. Thus it was that this youth (for he was now only nineteen years of age), by nature of a savage and impetuous temperament, became hurried into the execution of a desperate plot.

Unhappily for Mr. Cherry, he was but too little inclined to suspect treachery or violence on the part of the ex-nawaub, or to take those precautions which the case required. As the princely establishment and pretensions of Vizier Ali, according to the prejudices of the country, took him in some measure out of the control of the civil magistrate, and placed him under the immediate surveillance of the governor-general's agent, Mr. Cherry was the individual with whom the charge rested in the first instance. On the thirteenth of January, the native superintendent of police, who had been warned to be vigilant, waited on Mr. Davis, and reported to him that Vizier Ali was engaging a number of armed men in his service, and seemed to make no preparations for his departure to Calcutta. This was immediately communicated to Mr. Cherry, and the head of the police at the same time desired to watch the further movements of the parties.

Vizier Ali, when he had found all remonstrances vain, avowedly acquiesced in his proposed removal to Calcutta, and gave out that he should proceed on the fifteenth or sixteenth of January. On the night of the thirteenth, a hurcarrah, or messenger, came to Mr. Cherry's house and announced that the nawaub would visit him on the following morning, at breakfast. Early on the fourteenth another emissary came, and after making some inquiries, immediately returned. Some time afterwards Vizier Ali's drum was heard, and he was seen to approach with a train of horse and foot, consisting in all of about 200 men. In numbers this did not much exceed the retinue which he had been accustomed to move with; but a jemmadar of Mr. Cherry reported to his master, that this party, instead of coming in their usual manner, were all armed, and with matches lighted. Mr. Cherry, in reply, told the man that it mattered not, and that he was a fool for his fears.

On Vizier Ali's arrival, his host, according to custom, met and handed him in, accompanied by his friends, Waris Ali, Izzut Ali, and another, father-in-law to the last. Mr. Evans, a young private secretary, was also present. The party were attended into the breakfast room by four followers, armed with swords, shields, and pistols. When the chief persons had taken their seats, Mr. Cherry, calling for tea, handed it to Vizier Ali, who did not touch it; but, addressing himself to his host, said that he had something of great consequence to communicate. Then raising his voice, he began to complain of the treatment he had received from Sir John Shore, the late governor-general, who, he declared, had at first promised him six lacs of rupees per annum, but subsequently reduced it to a much smaller amount. 'On his departure,' continued Vizier Ali, 'Sir John Shore told me that you would take care of my interests, and attend to my representations; but this you have never done. On the contrary, at the suggestion of Saadut Ali Khan,* you now wish me to go to Calcutta; but Lord Mornington is absent—what should I do there? Saadut Ali Khan wishes for my death, and the English are in league with him. They listen to him; but neither you nor any one else attends to me. I shall therefore not proceed to Calcutta, but go where I please.'

While he was speaking, Waris Ali came round from his seat, and placed himself near Mr. Cherry. This seemed to be a concerted signal, for Vizier Ali, rising from his chair, seized Mr. Cherry by the collar, while the other held him behind, and, as he exclaimed against this violence, the nawaub struck at him with his drawn sword. The conspirators now followed the example set them, and as the unfortunate resident endeavoured to escape through the verandah into the garden, they followed him in a body, and cut him down before he had gone many yards on the outside.

In the meanwhile, Izzut Ali had seized Mr. Evans, and grasped at his dagger to stab him;

* The actual Nawaub of Lucnow.

but that gentleman, holding the assassin's hands, prevented his design. An attendant of the resident's now came up, and made a cut at Izzut Ali, which he received on his arm, and let go his hold of Mr. Evans, who fled into an adjoining field. There, however, he was seen by some horsemen, who, firing two or three shots, brought him to the ground, upon which some others of the conspirators ran up and dispatched him. Captain Conway, an officer who was living with Mr. Cherry, happened at this moment to ride up to the house, attended by an orderly, and he also was killed by the armed body.*

Mr. Davis, whose house was not much more than a quarter of a mile distant, in returning from his morning ride on an elephant, had passed Vizier Ali and his whole train, as they were proceeding towards Mr. Cherry's house; but their business was not with him *yet*—he providentially escaped, to be the instrument of saving many others. To him the train did not appear more numerous, nor in any respect different, from what he had often observed of

* See Appendix C.

them, except that they moved in rather closer order than usual. On reaching home, however, he found the cutwal, or head of the police, who stated that he had ascertained the fact of Vizier Ali having sent emissaries into the neighbouring districts to summon armed men, and that some mischief might be apprehended from his present visit to Mr. Cherry.

Mr. Davis immediately despatched a hasty note to Mr. Cherry, and being anxious for the return of his messenger, kept a look out in that direction; when presently he observed Vizier Ali and his train returning with much more haste than usual; and that some of the horse, instead of keeping the road, crossed into his grounds, and began firing at a sentry, stationed about fifty yards from the house, whom they shot down. There was now no time to lose. Mrs. Davis was told to repair, with her two children[*] and their attendants, to the terrace on the top of the house, while he himself ran for his firearms, which were below; but observing, on his way down, that an armed horseman was already in the doorway, he bethought him of a pike or spear,

[*] Of whom the writer of this was one.

which he had upstairs, and of the narrow staircase leading to the roof, which he considered defensible with such a weapon. The pike was one of those used by running footmen in India. It was of iron, plated with silver, in rings, to give a firmer grasp, rather more than six feet in length, and had a long triangular blade of more than twenty inches, with sharp edges. (Figured on this volume.)

Finding, when on the terrace, that the lowness of the parapet wall exposed them all to view, and that they were fired at by the insurgents from below, Mrs. Davis was directed, with her two female servants and the children, to sit down near the centre of the terrace, while Mr. Davis took his station on one knee at the trap-door of the stair, waiting for the expected attack. The perpendicular height of the stair was considerable, winding round a central stem. It was of a peculiar construction, supported by four wooden posts, open on all sides, and so narrow as to allow only a single armed man to ascend at a time. It opened at once to the terrace, exactly like a hatchway on board ship, having a light heading of mat covered with painted canvas stretched

D

on a wooden frame. This opening he allowed to remain uncovered, that he might see what approached from below.

In a few minutes, hearing an assailant coming up, he prepared to receive him. When full in view, and within reach with his sword drawn, the ruffian stopped, seeing Mr. Davis on his guard, and addressed him abusively. The only reply was—'The troops are coming from camp;' and at the same time a lunge with the pike, which wounded him in the arm.* The enemy disappeared, and Mr. Davis resumed his former position, when presently he observed the room below filled with Vizier Ali's people, and heard some of them coming up the stairs. At the first who appeared he again drove his spear, which the assailant avoided by warily withdrawing his person; but Mr. Davis, being by the action fully exposed to view from below, was fired at by the assassins. The spear, by striking the wall, gave the assailant on the stairs an opportunity of seizing the blade end with both his hands; but the blade being triangular, with sharp edges, Mr. Davis freed it in an instant,

* This proved to be Izzut Ali.

by dropping the iron shaft on the edge of the hatchway, and applying his whole weight to the extremity, as to a lever. The force with which it was jerked out of the enemy's gripe cut his hands very severely, as was subsequently observed from their bloody prints being left on the *breakfast table-cloth* below, where he had staunched them. There was blood likewise on the stairs, and some dropped about the floors of the rooms.

Though the present assailant disappeared like his predecessor, the repeated firing from below was discouraging, and Mr. Davis now thought it necessary to draw the hatch on, leaving such an opening at the edge as still admitted of his observing what was going on below. He saw them for some time looking inquisitively up, but not altogether liking the reception that there awaited them, one of the number went out to the verandah of the room, to see if they could get at Mr. Davis from the outside, while no further attempt was made on the staircase.

They presently withdrew in a body from the room, and were heard breaking the furniture and glass wall-shades. To this a silence and dreadful suspense succeeded; for though Mr. Davis could not quit his post for a moment to look out, the two women assured him the insurgents still surrounded the house, and it was a natural suggestion that they might be preparing the means of ascent on the outside. At length one of the women, venturing to look over the parapet wall, was shot through the arm by one of many who appeared like a guard stationed to prevent escape.

They could now only remain where they were, casting anxious looks for the cavalry from General Erskine's camp, which, though Mr. Davis doubted not it would hasten to his relief, he knew could not arrive for some time, not more than an hour having yet elapsed since the attack began. He maintained, however, that they must be at hand, for the sake of encouraging those whom he had to protect.

In about half an hour from this time, he again heard the noise of many persons ascending the stair in haste, and when by the sound they seemed near the top, he suddenly threw aside the cover, and was on the point of driving the spear into the head of the foremost, when most fortunately he recognised the white beard and withered face of an old native servant. The poor fellow, thinking himself endangered by this unexpected reception, roared out who he was, and that he had saved the piece of plate which he held up towards Mr. Davis, adding that Vizier Ali's force had all retired. Others behind in like manner held up different articles they had brought with them, to confirm his assertion; but Mr. Davis still hesitated for a moment to let them come up, for fear of treachery, not knowing but that they might have been tempted to save their own lives by consenting to be the means of putting him off his guard.

Presently, however, seeing the native officer of his police and some sepoys, with their muskets, enter the room, whose presence with their arms was alone sufficient to convince him that the enemy had retired, Mr. Davis gladly admitted this reinforcement to his post; and at length finding, on a muster, that he had fifteen men with their firelocks, bayonets, and fifteen rounds each, besides the cutwal with some of his police, he considered the danger as over; for though intelligence was now brought from the town by a police peon that Vizier Ali intended to renew his attack on the house, Mr. Davis had already found the roof of it perfectly defensible, and that those opposed to him understood better how to assassinate than to fight.*

He posted the soldiers, and instructed them as to the best mode of defence in case of attack, and they seemed steady and attentive to his directions. The sound of Vizier Ali's drum was presently heard from the town, and parties could be distinguished in motion about the suburbs, where some places belonging to Europeans were on fire. Intelligence was brought in that numbers of the inhabitants were joining the insurgents, but none of them yet approached the house.

About eleven o'clock an advanced party of cavalry appearing in view, every fear was dispelled from this little garrison. Major Pigot and Captain Shubrick, by whom it was brought on with admirable celerity, proceeded first over the bridge to Mr. Cherry's house. After finding all was over, they next galloped to Mr.

---

* For Lord Valentia's account, see Appendix D. There is also a succinct, but correct, statement in Thornton's History of the British Empire in India. 1843.

Davis's assistance. They there agreed that until the infantry arrived this small force would be best occupied by taking post in front of the house, within view of which, towards the town, great numbers were now beginning to assemble.

Whether these were mere spectators, or collected for a hostile purpose, remained uncertain, until some of the nearest of them began setting fire to a building attached to the police department. General Erskine, who by this time had joined with the remainder of the cavalry, sent out a few troopers to drive off these depredators, and one of the men, unfortunately falling from his horse, was set upon and left for dead by a part of the armed multitude, who by this proceeding evinced that they were of Vizier Ali's party. The cavalry were soon after fired at by some who, emboldened by their success over the trooper, came near enough for their shot to reach the verandah; and had not the column of infantry at this juncture come up, the party there assembled might have been much annoyed by the assailants.

The troops, while forming in line, were some

of them wounded by matchlocks or musket shot from a wood in their front, where Vizier Ali was said to be in person; but on the first fire from a field-piece he and his adherents withdrew towards Mahdoo Doss's garden, where it was thought a desperate resistance might be expected. General Erskine with the utmost promptitude pursued this column, leaving Mr. Davis a guard of a company of men, and from the verandah, where most of the European inhabitants were now assembled, they could see the smoke and hear the report of the firing which in due time succeeded.

At the first interval of breathing time the astonished assembly of English inhabitants of the neighbourhood felt and acknowledged that the hour and half during which Mr. Davis single-handed had kept the assassins at bay in their fruitless attack, had been the means of enabling some to conceal themselves, and others to take refuge in General Erskine's camp. The unfortunate victims to Vizier Ali's barbarous treachery, among the British, were five in number; for, in addition to Mr. Cherry, Captain Conway, and Mr. Evans, they had met Mr. Robert Graham, a young civilian, on their way to the attack on the judge and magistrate's house, and cut him to pieces; while Mr Hill, a European, who had a shop in the city, was also put to death. Some of the English made the best of their way to the camp, and others, especially those with families, concealed themselves as they could, and must probably have been discovered and massacred, if the attention of the insurgents had not been occupied by Mr. Davis's defence. One large party retired into a tall field of maize, or Indian corn, and were completely hidden for the time, though but a short distance from the residence of one of their number.

The recovery of the city was not effected without loss. The troops marched through one of the suburbs, and though the streets were wide, they suffered by the fire from the houses and the narrow lanes on each side. Among others killed, both of General Erskine's orderlies were shot at his side. On reaching Mahdoo Doss's garden, several shots from field-pieces were directed against the fortified house; but the most effectual operation was blowing open the gate by which the troops got admission to the principal court. This was effected just as the sun set. Had the contest lasted until dark, the town would in all probability have been pillaged by the numerous banditti and adventurers who were now assembled within its precincts.

Time would also have been given for adherents to have joined Vizier Ali from some of the neighbouring districts, and the final attack on his stronghold, at a later moment, might have been attended with considerably more loss than was actually experienced, situated as it was among narrow streets, and rendered much more defensible of late by the alterations made expressly for his accommodation.

When the troops got possession of the place, it was found that Vizier Ali had fled northwards, by the way of Azimghur, towards Betaul. He was accompanied by most or all of his horsemen, and a number of his armed foot followed in the course of the night. The next morning (fifteenth January) the Rajah of Benares, the two sons of the late eldest Shah-Zadah, or prince royal of Delhi, and many of the principal inhabitants of the city, waited on the judge and magistrate to evince their non-adherence to Vizier Ali; while another individual of the royal family, who for some time past had been itinerant in Hindoostan, sent an excuse for his having been seen with the assassins after their return to town from the massacre.

With respect to the Rajah himself, it soon became clear, on evidence given before Mr. Davis in court, that his attachment to the government was unshaken. A native servant of the collector of Benares being on his way to Beetabur, on the 14th, to give information to the army of Vizier Ali's proceedings, fell in with a party of the insurgent horse, headed by their chief himself. Three of the horsemen rode up to inquire who he was, and ended by taking his horse from him by force. The man being interrogated as to whom he served, replied with great adroitness that he was a servant of the Rajah of Benares. He then exclaimed aloud to Vizier Ali that he had come to him with a message from the Rajah, and that his horse had been taken from him. He added, that the Rajah had sent to demand intelligence concerning the present movement, and that if his horse was restored he would return with the answer.

Vizier Ali upon this gave the man a sealed letter, and told him to carry it to the Rajah of Benares; but, having thus cleverly escaped a very dangerous predicament, the messenger went straight to camp, and there delivered Vizier Ali's letter to the collector, who sent both the letter and the messenger to the judge and magistrate. The communication was to the following effect:—

'FROM VIZIER ALI KHAN TO RAJAH UDWUNT NARAIN SINGH.

' By the grace and bounty of God, the life of the worthless Cherry, who disturbed and oppressed you, the hereditary servant of my family, has been terminated by the warriors of the army of Islam. You, who are my hereditary servant and ancient well-wisher, whose ancestors were always ready with heart and soul for the service of my family, must consider these joyful tidings as the cause of your prosperity.

' Be ready with your people for my service, and guard well the roads about the city of Benares.

' Enjoin your people to permit no individual

of the British or other European nations to pass the boundaries of Benares, and to put all individuals of these nations, whose hiding-place they may discover, to death. Give also such directions as may prevent any person from crossing the river without my orders.

'I intend to cherish you more than your ancestors were cherished. The only wish of my heart is to protect you and my other subjects. Take care of your own places, and let your mind be perfectly at ease. Your wealth, honour, lands, and rank shall be increased more and more.'

It was clear that the Rajah had been wholly unconcerned in Vizier Ali's views, and that he never received the above letter; but as it soon came to his knowledge that a letter to himself from the ex-nawaub had fallen into Mr. Davis's hands, the latter thought it advisable to calm his apprehensions by the subjoined note in Persian :—

'A letter from Vizier Ali Khan, directed to you, was brought to me by Deha Singh, and the examination of the said Deha Singh was taken.

'Do not you be alarmed on this account, for though the nawaub wrote a letter to you, it is clear that you had no communication or correspondence with him; and I am well assured that you are a friend to the Company. I therefore write this to relieve you from any uneasiness that you may have felt on hearing the story of the nawaub's letter.'

It appeared from the evidence of a servant of the Rajah, that on the morning of the insurrection he was absent to the west of Benares on a hunting excursion, and that some horses belonging to him had been taken, during his absence, by force for the service of Vizier Ali. On resistance being made by his servants in charge, these persons had been severely maltreated by the insurgents, and fled for refuge to the Rajah himself.*

As a strong report prevailed that several baboos, or persons of rank, relations of the Rajah, but on unfriendly terms with him, were privy to the designs and confederates of Vizier Ali, it became Mr. Davis's duty to obtain such evidence as could be procured on the subject. The principal testimony was given by a Brah-

* See Appendix E.

min who had served Vizier Ali in the capacity of *astrologer*. Four months previous to the insurrection the ex-nawaub had said to this individual, ' Go to Juggut Singh (one of the baboos), and in case you find him well affected to me, tell him on my part that I intend to seize on the four zillahs (or districts) of Benares, and to make war against the English. Request him if he have any friendship for me to join us.'

This message being communicated to Juggut Singh, he replied, 'I am the slave of the nawaub, and ready to serve him. I will extend his dominions as far as Calcutta. Let me assemble troops and raise money from the bankers to defray the expense of massacring the English. I will then seize the bankers, extort money from them, and subdue the whole province.'

This being reported to Vizier Ali, gave him infinite satisfaction. He immediately delivered a pair of shawls, a sword, and a ring to the messenger, desiring him to convey them as a khelaut (or present) to Juggut Singh, and tell him that if he was the friend and confederate of the ex-nawaub to prepare himself. The other received the khelaut, and declared that he had prepared a list of sixty of his friends who would be ready to join them and take an oath of fidelity to the cause.

Expressing a wish at this time to have a private interview with Vizier Ali, Juggut Singh with some of his brothers was conveyed by night to a secret door belonging to the women's apartments. At this interview he gave a paper to the ex-nawaub, which the latter signed and returned, being probably some promise or contract in the event of their plot succeeding. At a subsequent meeting, the baboo declared his resolution to bring a force of many thousand men, well armed, and others undertook to do the same. When some one objected to the plot as hazardous, Juggut Singh exclaimed, ' I cannot live for ever ; how can I lose my life better than in the service of Vizier Ali.'*

The Brahmin who gave the above evidence

---

* Juggut Singh was a man of some talents, but of inordinate vanity. He possessed an excellent Persian library, and was proud of his poetical compositions in that language, which Mussulmans only could appreciate. This was not unlikely to have influenced him in relying on a chief of that religion for his aggrandisement. His delight was to repeat a compliment that had been paid him by a former nawaub, who called him ' the nightingale of India.'

and who acted the internunciary part in the detail, being for some reason or other set aside by Vizier Ali, resolved on giving information of the plot to Mr. Cherry; but that unfortunate gentleman, though he received a note from the Brahmin requesting an audience, declined seeing him, and took no further notice of the matter. It seemed as if his fate had been sealed from the first, and that no warnings could avail to rouse him to a sense of his danger.

Among that portion of the population of Benares which, immediately after the massacre at Mr. Cherry's house, had accepted Vizier Ali's pay, and joined him in a show of resistance to the troops, some met the fate they deserved on the spot; but no informations were at first laid that could warrant proceeding against particular individuals. In the general consternation which prevailed within the town, excited by the necessary operations of the troops (many of whose shot had entered it with fatal effect), as well as by the conduct of Vizier Ali and his followers, Mr. Davis deemed it most desirable to quiet the inhabitants by proclaiming the return of tranquillity, and inviting them to open their houses and resume their customary occupations.

He preferred this course to that of adding to their fears, and perhaps their disaffection, by an inquest after suspected persons; the more so, as many striking instances had occurred of a readiness to give information for the sole purpose of gratifying private resentment. He had, moreover, reason to believe, from the intelligence brought in, that most or all of those who had accompanied Vizier Ali to Mr. Cherry's house had by this time escaped from the town and were with him on his way to the north. For some days great alarm was kept up among the English, by their ignorance of the extent of the plot, and their recollection of the violence and duration of the former insurrection, in which Mr. Hastings had been exposed to so much danger.

By the 18th of January the public tranquillity seemed re-established, and as no apprehension remained of any further attempt to disturb it, the courts assembled for the despatch of business, and a circular letter was addressed to the civil authorities of the neighbouring districts, to obviate the ill effects of exaggerated reports arising from the late circumstances. Mr. Davis at the same time requested instructions from the supreme government in regard to the symptoms of confederacy with Vizier Ali, and of disaffection to the ruling powers manifested by the individuals already noticed, who, although nearly related to the rajah, were on unfriendly terms with him. A considerable quantity of evidence had likewise been obtained against certain zemindars of wealth and influence in the neighbourhood.

In applying for instructions as to the disposal of these, Mr. Davis strongly recommended that a special commission should be appointed, as it would carry the appearance of greater impartiality, and prove generally more satisfactory. were the trust committed to persons not resident in the district. The same commission might be authorised to decide the fate of certain of Vizier Ali's followers, who had been captured, and their confessions obtained ; as well as to consider the conduct of one personage of rank who had sent a written excuse for having been with Vizier Ali in arms.

On the day following the insurrection, some elephants, horses, and silver howdahs,* with other articles of less value, which the insur-

* Seats on the backs of elephants.

gents could not carry off with them, were seized and brought in by the troops and police. Respecting the disposal of these articles, instructions were required from the government; but the elephants, meanwhile, twenty in number, were sent into camp the morning after their capture, Mr. Davis having been informed by General Erskine of his want of cattle to carry the baggage and stores of the army.

In the plundering which succeeded to the massacre of Mr. Cherry and the other English gentlemen, some European inhabitants and a few of their native dependents suffered in their property, as the villains carried off everything that they thought would be useful to themselves. During the hour and a half in which they had vainly assayed to dislodge Mr. Davis from his stronghold, they had contrived to kill some of his native attendants, destroy the furniture of his house, carry away his serviceable horses, and shoot two which were pensioners, one of them having been a present from Warren Hastings.

What would have been his own fate, had they succeeded against him, plainly appeared from the following evidence and confession of a follower of the ex-nawaub:—'Vizier Ali Khan and his friends were up and armed all the night of the thirteenth. On the following morning they went to Mr. Cherry, and I went with them as far as the bridge, where I stopped. In two hours they returned, and after they had passed the bridge, an Englishman* coming that way in his palankeen was murdered by Vizier Ali's foot soldiers. When they came near the judge's house, Vizier Ali called out to his followers, that "he would give a horse and a thousand rupees to any one who would bring him Mr. Davis's head."' This, however, was not so easily to be had; and Mr. Davis happily lived to return the compliment with interest, as will appear from the following letter:—

'Sir,—I am directed by the Vice-President in Council to acknowledge the receipt of your letter of the fifteenth instant, and to express to you his deep concern at the melancholy events which have occurred at Benares. It is with the greatest satisfaction he learns that your gallant exertions were so successful in pre-

* Mr. Robert Graham.

serving yourself and family from the attempts of the assassins.

'I enclose for your information copies of the letters which have been written to the resident at Lucnow and Major-General Erskine. You are authorised to publish a reward of 20,000 rupees for the apprehension of Vizier Ali, alive or dead.

   (Signed)   'G. H. BARLOW,
           'Secretary to Government.'
'Fort William,
 20th Jan. 1799.'

The wife, and other females of Vizier Ali's family, amounting, with their attendants, to nearly one hundred persons, were all left by him at Mahdoo Doss's garden, his late residence and retreat. The women were treated with consideration, and the privacy of their apartments protected by the officer left in charge of the place on its capture. On application from General Erskine, Mr. Davis caused a daily allowance of provisions to be sent to them for their present subsistence, waiting the arrangements of government for their disposal.

One of the followers of the ex-nawaub, who had been captured subsequent to the retreat of his chief, gave in this evidence:—' When the British army arrived, Waris Ali said to Vizier Ali, that it was time to go to the gardens. They accordingly went and took post in the turret there. Subsequently, when cannon-shot were fired at the place, one of them hit the turret, and knocked down part of it; upon which Vizier Ali and Waris Ali came down armed, mounted their horses, and went through a small gate towards the north.' The conduct of Vizier Ali after the massacre, in formally proclaiming his government within the city, and his remaining there until forced out of it, sufficiently indicated his expectation of effectual assistance from the other conspirators in the neighbourhood; for under any other circumstances it is reasonable to suppose that he would not have risked the chance of being captured by delaying at all, but have fled at once. It was his rash experiment of putting the spirit of his confederates to the proof, at a time when the vicinity of the troops under General Erskine rendered it dangerous for them to act, that hastened his ruin. Though the baboos had proposed, with their followers, to stop or impede the advance of any force that might be sent to the relief of the town; yet they, like others, stood aloof, waiting the result of the massacre, when they might, according to circumstances, join the insurgents, or excuse themselves to government, under the pretence of their armed men having been entertained for their own security. This argument failed to avail them, since it appeared that at Pinderah, the men in question were assembled for some time prior to the fourteenth of January, the date of the insurrection, and that accordingly they must have been privy to the design, and acting upon it.[*]

It was further ascertained, on good evidence, that a nephew of Juggut Singh had come up from Sarun to Benares at his uncle's desire, and agreed to join him in the conspiracy, engaging to raise 20,000 men in Chupra and Barragong. The dissatisfied and restless disposition of this person had long been remarked by the public officers, and the present was not the first charge of a criminal nature in which he had been implicated. It was also clear that a chief, named Culb Ali Beg, otherwise known as Mogul Beg, had attended Vizier

[*] Appendix F.

Ali during the insurrection, and afterwards fled with him. The evidence against the zemindar, Bowannee Sunker, and his son Shoo Deo Singh, was equally conclusive, and perfectly agreed with their previous characters and conduct.

The extent and organization of the conspiracy were evinced by the statements of an European inhabitant, by name M‘Lean, resident at some distance from Benares, in the country. Soon after hearing of the massacre, about noon on the day of its occurrence, he had walked with two friends to the top of a large turret near his house, and was presently followed by certain zemindars, or native landholders, unknown to him. In talking over the melancholy event, the Englishmen reminded these zemindars of the peace and security which they enjoyed under the British Government, unexampled under their own despotic rajahs. Two other natives soon afterwards ascended the place with their swords and shields, joining in the conversation, and telling them that letters had been sent off to many persons of consequence, who might be expected that night with strong forces to join

Vizier Ali. One of them added that he himself had received an invitation to support the cause.

All these men talked in a high and insolent tone, blaming the British Government, and particularly the courts of justice, which they observed, placed the *great and low upon an equality*,* and with which all ranks were dissatisfied. The strange conduct and conversation of these men, added to what had occurred in the morning, naturally alarmed the Europeans, and the interview terminated in a demand of money on the part of the natives, which was accordingly promised, but never paid, as the speedy suppression of the insurrection rendered this needless.

After the flight of Vizier Ali, a number of papers were discovered containing lists of the forces which were to assist in his cause. One

---

* This very Oriental objection might almost lend a cast of seriousness to the jocose irony of Mr. Sydney Smith—'Every political institution, then, is favourable to liberty, not according to its spirit, but in proportion to the antiquity of its date; and the slaves of Great Britain are groaning under the trial by jury, while the freemen of Asia exult in the bold privilege, transmitted to them by their fathers, of being trampled to death by elephants.'—*Essays*, vol. i. p. 25.

of them ran as follows:—'I present for your information a list of those people whom I have attached to you, and bound by oaths to adhere to you. Of these there are two sorts; one consists of men who are ready in time of need to give up their lives in your service; the other is composed of persons who will join your army within five or six days after your first success.' The writer then adds a list of about four thousand eight hundred foot and a hundred horse, who would join Vizier Ali at once, with a further account of some eighty thousand who would subsequently espouse his cause. It appeared from all the accounts, that between two and three thousand actually composed the ex-nawaub's force on the day of the massacre. Mr. Mill relates, that 'the consternation of the reigning sovereign of Oude, when he heard that his rival and enemy had broken loose, was proportionate to the well-known weakness and timidity of his character. He regarded the insurrection at Benares as a conspiracy in which his subjects might themselves be concerned to any unknown extent. He suspected even his own troops, and requested Mr. Lumsden, the British resident at Lucnow, to call for the English battalion at Cawnpore, under the command of Colonel Russell, for the protection of his capital and person. When invited to join with his forces the British army, the effeminate Saadut Ali pleaded an excuse which his avarice, his timidity, his desire of ease and hatred of exertion, all contrived in leading him eagerly to adopt. He stated his suspicions of his troops, and represented them as too void, both of discipline and of fidelity, to be trusted; but he afterwards paid dear for this, when the representations of the moment were brought forward as reasons for quartering a British force in his dominions.'* Such is the representation of Saadut Ali's character, by the somewhat prejudiced, and not always correct historian of 'British India.' According to the testimony of a much higher authority—'Saadut Ali might have been timid, but he was not weak. He was a man of sense; kept up a degree of dignity and decorum in his court to which it had long been a stranger, and in his regular habits and application to business was more

* Mill's *British India*, vol. iii.

like an English gentleman than most natives. His vice was hard drinking ; but only at night. I speak of him as I saw him at Benares, and in the early part of his reign at Lucnow. I do not know what he was later in the day. He had good reason to be apprehensive of revolt, for his reign was new, and his natural parsimony, with the strict order and economy which he endeavoured to introduce into his provinces, were unfavourably contrasted with the profusion of his predecessors. The subsidiary force had been established by Mr. Hastings in 1775, and the augmentation now made had been agreed to before Saadut Ali left Benares.'—*Mountstuart Elphinstone.*

The resident at Lucnow communicated immediately by express with General Sir James Craig at Anopesher, and Colonel Russell at Cawnpore, with a requisition to the latter to march with his whole force to Lucnow. He likewise suggested to Sir James Craig the propriety of either returning without delay to that neighbourhood, or detaching such part of the army under his command as might suffice to crush all opposition ; more especially as certain intelligence had just been received of the retirement of Zemaun Shah from Lahore on his return home.

The nawaub was at the same time advised to issue circular orders to all his aumeels to be on their guard and seize the person of Vizier Ali, should he attempt to enter the territory of Oude; and as the detestation of his treacherous and bloodthirsty conduct seemed to be pretty general, it was hoped that he would soon be brought to the punishment due to his crimes. The city of Lucnow in the meanwhile continued in perfect tranquillity.

On the instant that it was ascertained at Benares that Vizier Ali had abandoned his defences and fled out from a gate at the back of the gardens, scouts were promptly despatched by the judge and magistrate to follow him if possible, and watch his movements. Nothing more was at first known of his flight than that it was in the direction of Azimghur, where it was not improbable that he might seek refuge, and meet with adherents. It subsequently appeared that he passed that place in haste, with only a few attendants, and after passing the Gogra at Doory Ghaut, retired towards Betaul,

a province belonging in part to the Nawaub of
Oude, and the remainder to the Rajah of Nepal.
Had General Erskine, at the moment of his
flight being known, even possessed authority or
deemed himself at liberty to pass the river and
enter the nawaub's dominions, it still appeared
problematical whether his following could be of
any use until some certain intelligence could
be obtained of the fugitive. It appeared that
he fled from Mahdoo Doss's garden, when the
field-piece opened against it, by a passage communicating from the back part into streets narrow and intricate; but the direction in which
he passed through the town, and the road he
afterwards took, were not known until late in the
evening, by which time he must have been at a
great distance from Benares. There was reason
to believe that the ex-nawaub and most of his
followers were mounted upon fresh horses; but
had it been otherwise, there was no probability
that any detachment which could have been
sent in pursuit could have overtaken him before he was out of the British territory.

At the moment when General Erskine's
column, in advancing to the attack on Mahdoo
Doss's garden, entered the suburbs, it had been

suggested to Mr. Davis by a native that a detachment might be sent by another route to intercept Vizier Ali's retreat; but the way which he took being at that time quite unknown, and having in his mind the fate of a detachment which, in Cheyte Singh's insurrection against Warren Hastings, was repulsed and almost destroyed by getting entangled in the narrow streets, Mr. Davis declined giving any hint, the consequences of which, by subjecting a part of the General's force to a similar situation, might render doubtful the success of the principal attack; more especially as he knew the proposed route to be very circuitous through narrow streets in a large city, which had just given signs of general hostility. To have marched the troops from Benares would have been extremely imprudent; for though apparent tranquillity returned when Vizier Ali had fled, yet strong suspicions of disaffection and conspiracy remained against certain persons of rank, and there was reason for feeling certain that Vizier Ali had adherents in many parts of the district who only waited for a favourable occasion to discover themselves.

For the present protection of the city and

district of Benares, Mr. Davis thought it necessary to make a requisition to General Erskine in the following terms:—

'From the evidence adduced before me, there is ground to suspect that some of the baboos distantly related to the Rajah of Benares had entered into the ultimate views of Vizier Ali, and that a zemindar in this neighbourhood actually collected armed men to second his operations. It is well known, and has been represented to government, that the city abounds with armed adventurers, who are ever ready to enter into any service at a moment's notice. There are in the district persons of rank who live and maintain their own guards without any limitation from government, and who are not under the same subordination to the laws as the other inhabitants; and although the danger resulting from these indulgences to individuals residing here is apparent in the use made of them by Vizier Ali, yet the same system must remain in force until the supreme government shall think proper to reverse or correct it. Under these circumstances, and so soon after the late insurrection, it would be the height of imprudence to leave the city of Benares destitute of a respectable military force; and six complete companies with two field-pieces are, in my opinion, the least that should be allotted for its protection.'

The encampment of General Erskine's force for some months in the immediate neighbourhood of Benares, ensured the district from a repetition of the late insurrectionary movements. In the meanwhile the supreme government of Calcutta sent instructions to Mr. Davis to take measures for securing the persons of certain Mahomedan nobles, known to be concerned in the attempt of Vizier Ali. In executing this service, two different modes presented themselves. The one by attachments in the usual form; the other by surprise with such a military force as should discourage resistance. Anything like an attempt to allure them into our power by civil invitations was justly spurned, as success itself only renders such treacherous measures, however consonant with Asiatic practice, the more disgraceful.

In the ordinary course of attachment, it could not be concealed from them that they were suspected persons, against whom informations had been taken, and concerning whose seizure instructions might be expected. It was most probable that they would have recourse to evasion or resistance, and in either case they might, with the assistance of their adherents, easily effect an escape, while to secure their papers would be impracticable. The Baboo Juggut Singh occupied a house capable of defence on the outskirts of the town, while three others usually resided together in the fort of Pinderah, distant about fourteen miles from Benares, on the Juanpore road. Bowannee Sunker and Sheo Deo resided in like manner at Chetaypore, a small fort on the Chunar side, until the former of the two disappeared, with the intention, it was supposed, of joining Vizier Ali, or remaining in concealment until his offences should be forgotten. Sheonaut occupied a small house in the town, with a few of the bravos so well known in Benares by the name of *Bankas*. They are of all castes, affect a peculiar way of dressing, half bully and half dandy, strut and swagger about the streets, and are always ready to pick a quarrel or to engage in any crime.

Under the circumstances it seemed advisable to plan the seizure of all these persons by surprise, at the same hour, lest the proceedings against one might alarm and enable another to escape. It was highly important, likewise, to secure possession of the two forts above mentioned, and especially that of Pinderah, which was surrounded by the family lands and old retainers of the proprietors, and, in case of insurrection ensuing from the measures in question, would afford a point of junction to their adherents.

As a regiment of infantry was then on its march from Lucnow to Benares, to join General Erskine's force, and must pass through Pinderah on its route, Mr. Davis addressed a requisition to the Major-General to this effect: 'In consequence of instructions I have this day received from the government, I am induced to request that you will be pleased to hasten the approach of the first regiment of native infantry, which I understand to be now on its march from Lucnow to Benares. I have also to request that the officer commanding the regiment be directed to halt, as if by accident rather than design, at Pinderah, on the Juanpore road, and that you will be pleased to in-form me, as soon as it can be ascertained, on what day we may depend on the arrival of the corps at that place. It is advisable that this communication, together with any instructions which you may issue in consequence, be kept as secret as possible.'

The Honourable Mountstuart Elphinstone, then a very young man, and assistant to the judge and magistrate of Benares, was deputed to meet Colonel Rayne, in command of the first regiment at Pinderah, and furnish him with authority to capture the parties implicated, in the event of their being in the fort; while that officer was instructed by the Major-General to use every exertion, not only in seizing the insurgents, but securing possession of the fort on account of the government.

On the 18th of March, Mr. Elphinstone was furnished by Colonel Rayne with four companies of infantry and twenty-four troopers to assist him in capturing the baboos. About daybreak the troops marched to the fort, and surrounded it in such a manner as to prevent any persons escaping. The fort was then entered, and every part of it searched, except the women's apartments. A large quantity of papers was discovered, and sealed up, together with a chest, said to contain money; but those in the fort declared that the baboos went out on the plea of hunting two days before, and had not returned since. A guard was placed over the zenanah, but it ultimately proved that they were not there. A seizure was made of fifty matchlocks, forty swords, and some powder and ball. The fort had lately been strengthened; and new walls with loopholes had been built on the side next the gate.

On the same morning, Mr. Sealey, another gentleman of the civil service, supported by two companies of infantry, proceeded at daybreak to the residence of Juggut Singh. On the first intelligence of the arrival of the troops, that delinquent retired to his zenanah, from whence he refused to come forth and surrender himself, though furnished with the summons, and assured of immunity from all personal violence and disgrace. His papers were secured with seals, and the officer in command surrounded the place with troops to cut off the means of escape.

The fate of another baboo, Sheonaut, was tragical, but such as his own conduct rendered inevitable. He shut himself up, with five adherents as desperate as himself, in a house, which with firearms and other weapons he rendered impregnable to the police. When one of these had been killed and another wounded with firearms from the windows and other apertures, a party of infantry surrounded the place, and stopped their supply of food and water. A whole day and night were spent in this manner, during which time every means was adopted to persuade them to surrender, and every assurance, both verbal and written, offered that no personal disgrace should be inflicted, but all without effect. They at length rushed out and attacked the assailants with fury. The chief and one of his companions were killed, but not before they had killed or wounded several of the force. The term *Banka*, by which this sect is distinguished, is derived from the peculiar movement of their swords, in the exercise of which they are proficients. This class of people formerly abounded in Benares, and were the terror of the wealthy and timid, on whose contributions, to avert enmity or secure regard, they were supposed chiefly to subsist.

Such being the fate of those adherents of Vizier Ali, whom he had left behind him in his flight, it remains only to trace the leader himself through his future fortunes to his ultimate destiny. The little resolution which he had shown, when pressed by General Erskine's force, probably discouraged many from joining or following him. He sought refuge beyond the British frontier at Betoul, and the forests under the first range of the Himalaya mountains. He there found himself in a short time at the head of several thousand men; descended with them into the plains of Goruckpore, the eastern district of Oude, and threw that kingdom into alarm. A British force was soon assembled to oppose him. Some partial rencounters, in which they suffered severely, and the narrow limits for subsistence or plunder to which they were reduced, soon disheartened his followers, when they abandoned him in great numbers, and Vizier Ali himself fled into Rajpootana, and took refuge with the Rajah of Jypore.

'The laws of hospitality are held so sacred in India,' observes Lord Valentia, 'that however disgusted the rajah might be with the crimes of

Vizier Ali, and however much he might wish to conciliate the British Government, he did not venture openly to surrender him; but on his being given up to Colonel Collins, attempted to throw the blame on his own minister. He actually imprisoned that functionary for some time for having, as he said, taken such a step without his consent. In justice, however, to the rajah, it would seem that he was influenced by no offers of reward, or any other unworthy motive, to give up the man who had claimed his protection. He stipulated for the life of Vizier Ali, and that he should not be confined by fetters.'

By a somewhat singular coincidence he passed the city of Benares as a prisoner on the first anniversary of the memorable insurrection and massacre, and being taken to Fort William, was lodged in a bomb-proof, divided by iron gratings into three parts. The largest, in the centre, was occupied by Vizier Ali, and the other two by sentries, one English and one native. In other respects, wherein security was not concerned, he was well treated. At length, after many years of captivity, he was transferred to a more suitable prison in the palace built for Tippoo Sultaun's family, in the fort of Vellore. There the females of his family subsequently joined him, and there he died.*

We may mention shortly the fate of the principal conspirators. Several fled the country. Juggut Singh and Bowannee Sunker were tried by a commission with unusual solemnity and condemned to death. The last named was executed; but Juggut Singh's sentence was commuted for transportation. He was sent down the Ganges to be embarked; but when he approached the sea he took poison, and escaped the loss of caste and other degradations he expected to suffer.

Lord Wellesley, who was Governor-General of India at the period of the insurrection of Benares, but absent for the time on a visit to Madras, subsequently expressed his sense of the defence made by Mr. Davis in a letter, wherein he attributed the safety of the English residents, and the salvation of the city from pillage, to the 'successful issue,' as his lord-

---

* Lord Teignmouth, in the Life of his father, lately published, states that Vizier Ali died in rigorous confinement in Fort William, but this is a mistake.

ship termed it, 'of that arduous trial of his prudence, activity and resolution.' The subsequent removal of that gentleman to Calcutta, the seat of supreme government, to fill offices of higher trust and importance, led to a personal friendship, which lasted through life, and was acknowledged by Lord Wellesley, shortly before his death, in a copy of the five volumes of his official despatches, which that distinguished statesman sent to the widow of his late friend, with this autograph inscription :—

'To Mrs. Davis, as a testimony of sincere respect and regard; and also a memorial of attachment, founded upon long intimacy, to the honourable and virtuous memory of her deceased husband; from her faithful friend and servant,
'WELLESLEY.'

SUPPLEMENT

BY THE

REV. JOHN LOCKWOOD,

Rector of Kingham, Oxon.

In the year 1798 the East India Company deposed Vizier Ali from the throne of Oude on account of his vices and cruelty; but gave him a splendid pension, and permitted him to take up his residence in the large and beautiful city of Benares, where he lived in almost regal splendour. It is said that he spent whole days and nights with the lowest associates, in revelry and drunkenness; on one occasion, enraged at a fall from a favourite horse, he ordered it to be burnt alive. To his great profligacy and cruelty, as is often the case with Orientals, he added great cunning; and perceiving among the chiefs of India a jealousy at the increasing power of the English, he determined to make use of it to regain, if possible, the throne from which he had been deposed.

He carried on his intrigues with great secrecy, and

obtained promises from many of the most powerful of the native princes, that they would render him assistance as soon as he should have commenced such a revolt against the English as would hold out any prospect of success. Relying on these promises, he increased his troops and retainers, and watched his opportunity to unfurl the standard of rebellion. But notwithstanding the secresy with which he carried on his plans, Mr. Davis, the chief magistrate of Benares, discovered that he was engaged in plots against the English, and wrote to the Governor-General, to advise that he should be immediately removed from Benares, where he was surrounded by chiefs and people of doubtful loyalty, and where he was so near the kingdom from which he had been deposed, as to be able to keep up a constant communication with it; and that he should be ordered to reside at Fort William, where all attempts to tamper with the fidelity of the native princes, or to spread discontent among the people, might be easily frustrated.

In consequence of this communication, an order was dispatched to the Vizier to leave Benares and proceed to Calcutta. He no sooner received this communication, than seeing that there was no time to be lost, he determined at once to put his plans into execution, and to commence his long-meditated rebellion; for he knew that if he once left Benares, the scene of action, and removed to Calcutta, he would be watched, cut off from his friends, and lose all hopes of success.

At that time there were many English residents at Benares, either as officials of the East India Company, or engaged in different branches of trade and commerce. The chief of these were Mr. Cherry, the resident, and Mr. Davis, the judge and first magistrate, whose houses were about a mile without the city gates; and three miles, again, beyond them, were large cantonments, containing a brigade of the Anglo-Indian army.

On the 14th of January, 1799, soon after his order of removal, the Vizier commenced his revolt. Leaving a large force in the city, he proceeded, with 200 chosen men, to the house of Mr. Cherry, under the pretence of paying him a friendly visit, but with the real purpose of putting him to death; and on his way thither he fell in with Mr. and Mrs. Davis, returning from their usual morning ride on an elephant. The instant he saw them he held a short consultation with his friends, whether he should at once attack and kill them on the spot, or should leave them for the present; and it was decided that as they did not appear to have any suspicion of his intentions, it would be better to proceed first to the house of the Resident, which was farthest from the city, and take them in his way back.

Mr. Davis at once perceived that the Vizier was engaged in some treacherous and hostile design, but thought it best to conceal his opinion; and having received and returned the salutation of the party with apparent indifference, he hastened home, and immediately dispatched a messenger to Mr. Cherry, to warn him of some impending danger. But it was too late. Already had the unfortunate Resident and his friends fallen beneath the swords of the Vizier and his soldiers; and before any escape could be effected, or any preparation be made for defence, they were seen hastening towards Mr. Davis's house. What was be done? Who were to be trusted? Were the native servants in the plot? Should they resign themselves at once to despair, and perish without a struggle? Mr. Davis possessed a bold and master spirit; but what could the courage of one man, however resolute, without a weapon, avail against two hundred troops armed to the very teeth. It was a moment of agony; but Mr. Davis at once perceived the only hope of safety, though that hope was a forlorn one.

In India the roofs of the houses are flat, and ascending to the roof of his own house was a narrow spiral staircase, with a trap-door at the top made with strong bamboo and thick matting, which let down upon the entrance. Up this staircase he urged his trembling wife and a Portuguese nurse, with one of his two little children in her arms;—but where was the other? His wife ventured down to seek for it, but was soon obliged to return, having scarcely escaped the pursuit of armed men. But what was her joy when she met, at the top of the stairs, the child whom she had sought at the peril of her life. Mr. Davis soon followed, taking with him a long and formidable spear, which he had snatched from the hands of a native servant, whose office it was— according to Eastern custom—to wait with it before his master's door, ready to accompany any of the family in their palanquin.

The Vizier, after searching the lower part of the house without finding the inmates, ordered some of his men to mount the spiral staircase. On the roof, at the top of the stairs, stood Mr. Davis, the trap-door partially lifted up, and the spear in his hand; and the instant the first man turned the angle, with a vigorous thrust—to which the fearful peril of his position added energy—he threw him wounded down the stairs. Another and another followed, forced on by the Vizier, but with the same result; firing their pistols up the stairs in hopes of hitting the brave defender. But fortunately the thick matting of the trap-door proved to be bullet proof. Unable to gain the roof, the Vizier now paused; but presently ordered one of his strongest men to watch his opporunity and seize the spear. He did so. But by making a prop of the trap-door, Mr. Davis with a sudden jerk drew it back, almost cutting in two the man's hands with the sharp sides. Another pause ensued; and the nurse venturing to look over the parapet to discover the cause, received a bullet in her arm; for men had been placed in different situations, with orders to fire at anyone they could catch sight of on the roof.

Nearly an hour had now passed since the Vizier had entered the house; when presently a well-known voice was heard on the stairs, and an old grey-headed native servant ascended with the news that the Vizier and his men were gone. The first impression upon Mr. Davis was, that the old man had been forced to act a traitor's part, and that from behind him would rush armed men; but being convinced of his fidelity, he admitted him to the roof, as well as some others who had come from their hiding-places. It was now ascertained that the Vizier had withdrawn his men to a little distance, and had dispatched some of them to the city, no doubt for the purpose of obtaining ladders to scale, or materials to fire, the house.

The only hope now of the besieged was, that the news of the revolt had reached the cantonment, and that assistance would arrive before it was too late. It was a state of fearful suspense; but before long they heard the distant trampling of horses. Was it the Vizier returning? or was it their friends coming to their rescue? Mr. Davis shut down the trap-door, and approached towards the parapet; and a burst of joy proceeded from the whole party as they perceived a regiment of cavalry, headed by English officers, galloping towards the house.

It appears that Mr. Cleves, a deputy judge, seizing the opportunity while the Vizier was at Mr. Davis's, mounted his horse, and by a circuitous route, to avoid meeting any of the conspirators, reached the barracks in safety, just as a regiment of cavalry were returning from their morning exercise. Not an instant was to be lost. Major Shubrick, who commanded, gave the order, and immediately the whole force turned their horses' heads, and hastened to the rescue; leaving Mr. Cleves to make his communication to the general, who instantly ordered out the troops; and a considerable force soon marched from the encampment, taking the road towards Mr. Davis's house, where they left on their arrival a guard, and then proceeded onward to the city. In their way thither they were attacked by the Vizier, who had been joined by his forces, and had taken up his position in a wood to the left; but being dislodged by artillery, he retreated to the town, and proceeded to his own residence called Mahdoo Doss's Garden, which had previously been fortified, and prepared against attack. The English followed and suffered considerable loss, from being fired at from the houses. But they soon made a breach in the walls, and the gates also being forced, they entered the courts of the garden just as the sun set.

The Vizier made a precipitate retreat, accompanied by a large body of troops. With these he entered the district of Betoul, where he collected an army of some thousands; but being attacked by the English, and defeated, he fled to Rajpootana, and took refuge with the Rajah of Jypore. By the Rajah he was given up to the English, on condition that his life should be spared, and that he should not be bound by fetters. He was brought down to Calcutta, and was placed in what could hardly be called otherwise than an iron cage; from thence, after a time, he was removed to the Fort of Vellore, where he died.

But to return to Mr. Davis. On descending from the roof of the house, he found the furniture of the lower rooms destroyed; the mirrors, which were of considerable value, broken; and the table-cloth, which had been laid for breakfast, awaiting his return from his morning ride, covered with blood from the wounds of the discomfited invaders of the roof. And without the house, to his great grief, he found three faithful native servants, either dead or dying of their wounds; with two old horses (which had formerly belonged to Warren Hastings, but were given to Mr. Davis, with a request that he should take care of them, as old and favourite servants) lying dead before the stables, where they had been shot by the Vizier; the other horses being conveyed away.

The painful task now fell upon Mr. Davis, as judge and chief magistrate, to enter into an investigation of the conspiracy, and see how far it had extended, and what native princes had been engaged in it. He found that the plan of the Vizier had been, first, to murder the Resident and the Judge, with their households, so that none could escape to make known the revolt to the English army ; and then to massacre the English residing within the city, and closing the gates, arm the townspeople ; and the city once in a state of defence, and the English inhabitants destroyed, he thought it would give such hopes of success that the native princes would be induced to fulfil their promises, and join his standard. But the long delay at Mr. Davis's disconcerted all his plans, and brought the English forces upon him before his scheme was sufficiently well prepared.

Many native princes and nobles were found to be implicated in the conspiracy, and long lists were discovered of forces which were to have been sent to his assistance; and had not Vizier Ali been prevented carrying his plans into execution by the brave defence of Mr. Davis, it is impossible to say what might have been the result—with the French ready to take every advantage, and the Mahomedan princes anxious to regain their power and expel the infidel from the land. But, as is often the case, because the rebellion was so soon terminated, men looked not beyond; and he who by his bravery saved the settlement of Benares, and arrested a conspiracy that might have spread like wildfire and jeopardised the whole of our Indian possessions, only received (in the absence of Lord Wellesley at Madras), a cold letter of thanks from the Council at Calcutta. But to this day, among the natives, the affair of Benares, and the disappointment of the Mahomedan princes, is still fresh in remembrance; and when the natives would show the effects of bravery, and that, however great the odds, none should despair, they relate how Davis Sahib and his spear kept at bay 200 armed men, with a prince at their head.

And having now brought this history to a conclusion, it only remains to give a brief sketch of the career of the brave man who played so conspicuous a part in it.

Mr. Davis went out to India as an engineer officer in the Company's service, but with the privilege, occasionally granted in those days, of leaving the army if he wished it, and becoming a civilian. The first station he went to was Madras; and here he became aide-de-camp to the commander-in-chief, and went with him to Calcutta, where, soon after his arrival, he was appointed, from his known talents for surveying, to accompany Mr. Turner in his embassy to Thibet. During this expedition he made a large collection of excellent plans and coloured drawings, the latter of which are still valuable, not only as accurate representations of that country, its temples and buildings, but as beautiful works of art.

On his return to Calcutta, thinking that the civil service afforded more prospect of advancement, he left the army, and obtained the appointment of collector of Burdwan; and while in this situation he married Henrietta, daughter of Mr. Boileau, of Dublin, whose ancestor—of the ancient family of the Barons de Castelnau, in Languedoc—had left his native country at the Revocation of the Edict of Nantes, and settled in Ireland. He had not been long at Burdwan before he was removed to Benares, to act in the position of judge and chief magistrate over that district. And being an excellent linguist and astronomer, he no sooner took up his residence in the holy city of the Hindoos than he became acquainted with the Brahmins of the highest caste; and particularly with one who gave him much valuable information respecting both the ancient religion and astronomy of the Hindoos. This Brahmin was afterwards proved by undoubted testimony to have been actively engaged in Vizier Ali's rebellion, and was brought up for judgment before Mr. Davis. The judge, seeing his old friend, could not contain his emotion, and the tears fell from his eyes as he heard the proud Brahmin express his readiness to die, but entreat that he might not be degraded, or anything done to him unworthy of his high caste and station.

Shortly after this he was summoned to Calcutta, to carry into execution some plans connected with the public revenue; and when he had accomplished these, he left for England, having formed an intimate friendship with the three most distinguished men connected with India during his residence there—Warren Hastings, Sir W. Jones, and the Marquis Wellesley. The latter of these showed in what high esteem he held his memory, by the autograph inscription—already given at p. 75—written in a copy of his Dispatches, which he presented to the widow of his friend.

Soon after his arrival in England he entered into the direction of the East India Company; and being requested by a Committee of the House of Commons to draw up a report upon the state of the revenues of India, he wrote that very able treatise known as *The Fifth Report*. But the labour of finishing this in a perfect state, within a limited period, accelerated a disease already latent in his constitution; for not long afterwards he was taken ill, and gradually growing weaker under the effects of a painful disorder, he died the 16th day of June, 1819, at his house at Croydon, in the 59th year of his age.

APPENDIX.

A. BENARES.

'THE city of Benares is so holy that several Hindoo Rajahs have habitations there, in which their vakeels (ministers or agents) reside, and perform for them the requisite sacrifices and ablutions. The land is extremely valuable, and lawsuits respecting it most frequent.

'The mosque, with its minarets, was built by Aurungzebe to mortify the Hindoos. Not only is it placed on the highest point of land, and most conspicuous from being close to the river, but the foundations are laid on a sacred spot where a temple before stood, which was destroyed to make room for it. This edifice violated the holy city, and proudly overlooked all the temples, and, what was perhaps more galling, all the terraces of the houses where the females were accustomed to enjoy the cool of the morning and evening.'—*Lord Valentia*, vol. i. p. 105.

B.

'In the progress of this revolution many circumstances occurred to create doubt and anxiety. The failure of the post, the interception of my letters, any irresolution on the part of Saadut Ali, or accident in the course of his journey to Khanpoor, might have involved me in serious embarrassments. As it was, I had a difficult task to amuse all parties, so as to prevent the discovery of my plans. The confidence which I was obliged to place in many was in no instance violated; and the declaration of my intention to place Saadut Ali on the musnud, after his arrival at Khanpoor, was a surprise to all who were not in my confidence. But, above all, I owe unbounded gratitude to Providence, which enabled me to accomplish so great a revolution without the loss of lives, and contrary to the expectations of almost all who knew my plans. Assassination, contempt of the Engglish, and the power of Vizier Ali to resist them, were the common topics of conversation amongst the desperate crew who attended the confidential hours of Vizier Ali. It was a surprise to all that they did not succeed in instigating him to some act of desperation, with a view to avail themselves of the confusion to plunder the town. The Vakeel of Ambagee, a Mahratta chieftain, who arrived at Lucnow on the

15th of the month, had an opportunity of learning the projects entertained by the adherents of Vizier Ali, viz. to raise a commotion, plunder the city, and retire with the spoils into the Mahratta frontier. They were heard to remark that if a single shot were fired it would be sufficient, and that thousands would be sacrificed. Every street in Lucnow was filled with armed men; and the accumulation of them on the 19th and 20th was observed by several Europeans. During the three successive days from the 21st great numbers were seen returning from the town, and passing the English camp in the neighbourhood. The consequence of an armed opposition in such a town as Lucnow would have been shocking. It is computed to contain 800,000 inhabitants; and the streets are, for the most part, narrow lanes and passages. Ibrahim Beg had under his charge about 300 pieces of ordnance, of which sixty or seventy were fit for immediate use; they were served by 1,000 Gole andages, or native artillerymen; and the number of artillery drawn out for apparent opposition consisted of thirty pieces, so posted that they could not be seized without great slaughter. Ibrahim Beg, the commandant, was a violent and hot-headed Mogul, regardless of any authority, fearless of his own life, and careless of the lives of others. The single accident which happened had, in all probability, no connexion with the revolution. The successful accomplishment of it was to me a relief from more anxiety than I ever before experienced.'—*Lord Teignmouth's Narrative.*

C.

'The massacre at Benares was by some supposed to have been a mere ebullition of rage in Vizier Ali on finding that he must go down to Calcutta; and that his resentment against Mr. Cherry was owing to that gentleman having so ably arranged the journey of Saadut Ali to Cawnpore, when summoned by Sir John Shore to be placed on the musnud, that his departure was not suspected by his own family until they heard of his having reached his destination. That this may have heightened his dislike to Mr. Cherry may be believed; but it is evident that his plan of insurrection was arranged long before the arrival of the order for his removal, which in fact was not issued until after repeated warnings had been received by the government that he meditated mischief. The Nawaub Vizier made strong representations on the subject to the resident at his court, which were communicated to Mr. Cherry. So convinced was General Erskine of the danger, that he urged Mr. Cherry to have a few companies of sepoys stationed at Seerole, but without success. The massacre had been evidently determined on when the assassins quitted

Mahdoo Doss's garden, for, according to the Mussulman superstition, they carried with them their winding-sheets, which had been dipped in the holy well at Mecca.'—*Lord Valentia*, vol. i. p. 113.

D. The Domestic Thermopylæ.

'I examined the staircase that leads to the top of the house, and which Mr. Davis defended with a spear for upwards of an hour and a half, till the troops came to his relief. It is of a singular construction, in the corner of a room, and built entirely of wood on a base of about four feet. The ascent is consequently so winding and rapid that with difficulty one person can get up at a time. Fortunately, also, the last turn by which you reach the terrace faces the wall. It was impossible, therefore, to take aim at him while he defended the ascent with a spear; they, however, fired several times, and the marks of the balls are visible in the ceiling. A man had at one time hold of his spear, but by a violent exertion he dragged it through his hand, and wounded him severely. This gallant defence saved the settlement, as it gave time for the cavalry, which were quartered at Beetabur, about ten miles from Benares, to reach Secrole, and oblige Vizier Ali to retire with his followers to his residence in Mahdoo Doss's garden.'— *Lord Valentia*, vol. i. p. 108.

E.

Among the papers of Vizier Ali was found this letter from the brother of the Nawaub of Dacca to Zemaun Shah, conjuring him to place himself at the head of the Mussulman league, and free India from the British:
—'From the beginning the decrees of Providence have so ordered, that when the affairs of the world are changed, and in a ruinous state, the divine greatness selects some one particularly favoured by heaven, assists him, and extends his power over the world, that mankind may prosper by his just administration. In these times, when disorder rears her head to the skies, and religion as well as worldly concerns are in the greatest confusion, the Almighty Disposer of Events has placed your illustrious majesty on the throne, that you may give peace to mankind and improve their condition. Considering your majesty as the support and champion of the true faith, I am happy to offer my services in the most zealous manner, and rank myself among the propagators of our holy religion. Such is the desire of my heart, and my religious zeal, that I observe and presume to represent, in an open and unreserved manner, the evils under which this country labours, and to state to your majesty my own wishes. However great were the obstacles to my submitting myself to your majesty's protection, I have at length fortunately

surmonnted them, and, trusting to Providence, have dispatched this letter to your majesty's court by Sheik Ali, of Amil, who will explain fully all circumstances relating to this country. I hope your majesty will be pleased to hear him. I beg leave to observe, that owing to the imbecility of the house of Timour, and the contempt into which it has fallen of late years, the powerful have been weakened and the weak become powerful. Worthless unbelievers and ambitious villains have started up from every corner, boldly conquered all these countries, and established themselves here. As the poet observes, 'When the lions leave the plain, the jackals become bold.' For these reasons religion, which should be so highly prized, is here lost and of no value; nothing of Islamism remains but the bare name. They have so stripped and reduced the principal Mussulmans, that they have no resource, and are obliged implicitly to obey their orders. The Mussulmans have become vile and wretched; the honour of the great men is gone. Christians seize and keep by force the daughters of Syeds and Mussulmans. Under these circumstances, when we can no longer act openly, it behoves us to exert ourselves secretly in the cause of religion. If your majesty's victorious standard shall be directed towards these parts for the establishment of religion and destruction of its enemies, by God's assistance your majesty will in a short time, and without any difficulty, conquer this country and annihilate your enemies. I hope your majesty will be graciously pleased to number me among your attached slaves.'

F.

'On Sunday the 13th, when an hour and a half of the day remained, I with my own eyes saw Sheo Deo Singh and Bowannee Sunker going from their house to the village of Koondnah, with two hundred men armed with guns and swords. Sheo Ruttan said to Hurdeal and me, "These men used not to have above ten or twelve attendants; where and for what purpose are they now going with such a crowd?" On this Hurdeal and I went and mixed with the multitude and accompanied them to a tank, on the bank of which there is a temple of Mahadeo, where they sat down and conversed with twelve of their companions, saying that they would halt there for that day, and that on the night of the next day they would surprise the troops at Beetabur. Then the two leaders called their people, and said that they had promised and engaged to Vizier Ali to surprise the troops at Beetabur on the following night. They then offered their people four rupees apiece, but they refused them, and said, " You promised us eight rupees apiece; we will not take less." When four or five hours of the night were past, five or six horsemen came at a gallop. When they came near, every person who was present rose up, and Bowannee Sunker and Sheo Deo Singh joined the horsemen, and went with them to the temple of Mahadeo, on the side of the tank. These people say that they consulted about attacking the camp at Beetabur. After the conversation, the horsemen went towards the city. I asked their servants who they were, and they said that it was the nawaub Vizier Ali. Afterwards the chiefs told their companions of its having been settled, in their conversation with Vizier Ali, that they should prevent any forces coming while he was fighting the English gentleman, and that they should engage the troops from Beetabur. They besides said to their companions, "Vizier Ali has given us money to assemble troops, also khelauts and horses; and if he conquer the British he will do much for us, as well as for you, and we will give you the employment of jummadars." On Monday, after Mr. Cherry's death, when the cavalry were approaching Nundaisur, one horseman in galloping away was pursued by the cavalry, upon which he threw himself from his horse and went and hid himself in the house of a servant of Mr. Williams, who resides there. The horseman was delivered up to the cavalry, who carried him away. When the infantry arrived, Shoo Deo Singh set off, with fifty horse, for Ramnaghur, and Bowannee Sunker went I know not whither.'— *Evidence.*

www.ingramcontent.com/pod-product-compliance
Lightning Source LLC
Chambersburg PA
CBHW030052170426
43197CB00010B/1497